Owls

ABDO
Publishing Company
A Buddy Book
by
Julie Murray

VISIT US AT
www.abdopub.com

Published by Buddy Books, an imprint of ABDO Publishing Company, 4940 Viking Drive, Suite 622, Edina, Minnesota 55435. Copyright © 2005 by Abdo Consulting Group, Inc. International copyrights reserved in all countries. No part of this book may be reproduced in any form without written permission from the publisher.

Printed in the United States.

Edited by: Christy DeVillier
Contributing Editors: Matt Ray, Michael P. Goecke
Graphic Design: Maria Hosley
Image Research: Deborah Coldiron
Photographs: Corbis, Corel, Digital Stock, Photodisc

Library of Congress Cataloging-in-Publication Data

Murray, Julie, 1969-
   Owls/Julie Murray.
      p. cm. — (Animal kingdom. Set II)
   Contents: Birds of prey — Owls — Where they live — Their body — Size and color — What they eat — Barn owls — Snowy owls — Babies.
   ISBN 1-59197-328-7
      1. Owls—Juvenile literature. [1. Owls.] I. Title.

QL696.S8M87 2003
598.9'7—dc21

                                                    2003040384

Contents

Raptors

Raptors are strong, meat-eating birds. Most raptors hunt for their food. These birds have hooked beaks and sharp claws. A raptor's sharp claws are called **talons**. Owls, eagles, hawks, vultures, and falcons are all raptors.

Raptors are strong birds with hooked beaks.

Owls

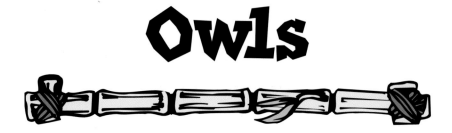

Long ago, people thought owls were wise. Others thought owls were bad luck. Today, people know that this is not true.

There are more than 160 kinds of owls. They belong to one of two owl families. One family is the barn owls. Barn owls have a heart-shaped face.

Typical owls belong to the other owl family. Most typical owls have a round face.

A barn owl (left) and a typical owl (right).

What They Look Like

Owls are brown, gray, or white. Many have spots or stripes.

The great gray owl is one of the largest owls. It grows to become almost three feet (one m) tall.

One of the smallest owls is the elf owl. Adults are only about six inches (15 cm) tall.

Owls fly with large wings. Their wing feathers are soft along the edge. These wing feathers allow owls to fly very quietly. This helps owls catch **prey**.

Owls have large wings.

Owl Eyes

Many owls see very well in the dark. They have big, round eyes. Owls cannot move their eyes like people can. An owl must move its head to see in other directions.

Where They Live

Owls live on every continent except Antarctica. They live in forests, mountains, deserts, grasslands, and wetlands. Most owls stay in the same area all year long. Some fly south for the cold winter months.

A great horned owl in its nest.

Owls do not build their own nests. They often use empty nests built by other birds. Owls nest in trees, hollow logs, empty buildings, and barns. Some owls nest in the ground, too.

Burrowing owls nest in the ground.

Hunting And Eating

Owls are **predators**. They hunt and eat other animals. Keen hearing and eyesight helps owls catch **prey**. They fly very close to animals. Then, owls catch the prey with their strong feet and **talons**.

Some owls hunt more at night. Others hunt during the day. Owls often hunt pests that eat farm crops. Some of these pests are rabbits and rats. Owls also eat mice, squirrels, insects, and fish.

This barn owl has caught a mouse.

Owls commonly eat small **prey** whole. If it is too big, they tear their food into pieces.

An owl's stomach cannot break up bones and fur. These things form a **pellet** in the owl's stomach. An owl spits up the pellet about 12 hours after eating. Scientists study these pellets to learn more about owls.

Barn Owls

Barn owls are sometimes called "ghost owls." They have a white face. Barn owls hunt at night. They can eat more than 1,000 mice in a year.

Not all barn owls live in barns. They nest in caves, hollow trees, and windmills, too.

Barn owls have a white face.

Snowy Owls

Some snowy owls have white feathers all over. Feathers cover their legs, too. These all-white owls match the snow. Other snowy owls are white with brown spots.

Snowy owls live in cold parts of Canada and Alaska. They sometimes **migrate** south for the winter. Snowy owls nest on dirt mounds. They mostly hunt during the day.

Snowy owls have white feathers.

Owlets

Female owls can lay as many as 12 eggs. But most owls lay three or four eggs. A mother owl sits on her eggs to keep them warm. Keeping eggs warm is called **incubation**. The eggs hatch after three to five weeks.

Baby owls are called **owlets**.
Newborn owlets have white, fluffy fur.
Their eyes open after about seven days.

Owlets are white and fluffy.

Mother and father owls bring food to their babies. They teach the **owlets** to fly and hunt. After three months, the young owls leave their parents. Owls can live as long as 25 years.

Owlets learn to hunt and catch prey.

Important Words

incubation keeping eggs warm until they hatch.

migrate to move from one place to another when the seasons change.

owlet a baby owl.

pellet what owls spit up many hours after eating.

predator an animal that hunts other animals.

prey an animal that is food for another animal.

raptor a large, meat-eating bird with sharp talons and a hooked beak.

talons the long, hooked claws of raptors.

Web Sites

To learn more about owls, visit ABDO Publishing Company on the World Wide Web. Web sites about owls are featured on our Book Links page. These links are routinely monitored and updated to provide the most current information available.

www.abdopub.com

Index